I Have a Question about Cancer

in the same series

I Have a Question about Divorce
Clear Answers for All Kids, including Children with Autism
Spectrum Disorder or other Special Needs
Arlen Grad Gaines and Meredith Englander Polsky
ISBN 978 1 78592 787 4
eISBN 978 1 78450 734 3

I Have a Question about Death
Clear Answers for All Kids, including Children with Autism
Spectrum Disorder or other Special Needs
Arlen Grad Gaines and Meredith Englander Polsky
ISBN 978 1 78592 750 8
eISBN 978 1 78450 545 5

of related interest

Big Tree is Sick
A Story to Help Children Cope with
the Serious Illness of a Loved One
Nathalie Slosse
Illustrated by Rocio Del Moral
ISBN 978 1 78592 226 8
eISBN 978 1 78450 509 7

I Have a Question about Cancer

Clear Answers for All Kids, including Children with Autism
Spectrum Disorder or other Special Needs

Arlen Grad Gaines and Meredith Englander Polsky

Jessica Kingsley Publishers
London and Philadelphia

First published in 2019
by Jessica Kingsley Publishers
73 Collier Street
London N1 9BE, UK
and
400 Market Street, Suite 400
Philadelphia, PA 19106, USA

www.jkp.com

Library of Congress Cataloging in Publication Data
A CIP catalog record for this book is available from the Library of Congress

British Library Cataloguing in Publication Data
A CIP catalogue record for this book is available from the British Library

ISBN 978 1 78592 694 5
eISBN 978 1 78592 842 0

Printed and bound in China

For Abigail

Acknowledgements

With much gratitude to Suzanne Adelman, Dr. Robert A. Beckman, Abigail Bortnick, Jamie Dashoff, Wendy Fischman, Dr. Caren Glassman, Rae Grad, Jessica Rogers, Manny Schiffres, Aviva Seiden, and Dr. Michael Westerman.

We could not have written this book without the generosity of the parents who shared their personal experiences and trusted us with their stories.

Thank you to Elen Griffiths, Simeon Hance, and the staff at Jessica Kingsley Publishers for their continued encouragement and guidance.

Our heartfelt thanks to our families for their constant support.

Preface

Cancer is a difficult topic for parents to explain to any child, perhaps even more so when the child has Autism Spectrum Disorder or other special needs. Many of these children process information in a concrete manner, prefer established routines, and need support understanding and interpreting emotions. We wrote *I Have a Question about Cancer* to provide a straightforward resource that takes these considerations into account and seeks to cover the wide range of questions that emerge as children learn that someone in their life has cancer.

This book reflects actual questions that children have asked as they are learning that someone they love has been diagnosed with cancer. As an introduction to the topic, we hope this book will lay the foundation for additional conversations, whether about a particular type of cancer, how cancer is treated, or other challenges that emerge.

We believe that special education is just *really good* education and hope that this book, and the strategies contained within, serves as a resource for all children.

I Have a Question about Cancer consists of three components:

1. The complete story
Created with straightforward text and clear illustrations for children who process information best through words and pictures.

2. Short picture story
Designed for children who learn best through visual cues, and for those who may want to re-read the story and think about it independently.

3. Suggestions for parents and caregivers
Provides ideas for parents and caregivers in supporting a child, including one with special needs, through the process of finding out a loved one has cancer.

Hi! I'm a kid who likes a lot of things. I like playing games, going swimming, and watching my favorite show.

I'm also a kid who likes to know what to expect each day. Most of the time that works out fine.

Most days are regular days. They go like this:

I wake up. I have breakfast. I brush my teeth and my hair. I get dressed for school and I walk to the bus.

I see my teachers and friends and work hard.
In the afternoon, I come home, do my homework,
and play at my house. I eat dinner, take a shower
(most nights!), and go to sleep.

Once in a while, though, something different happens and the day doesn't go the way I expect.

Today was one of those days. I learned something new. I learned that someone I love has cancer.

I really wasn't expecting that.

Now I have a lot of questions. I'm a kid who likes when there are answers to my questions. Today, I'm asking my questions and some of them have answers. But some of them don't.

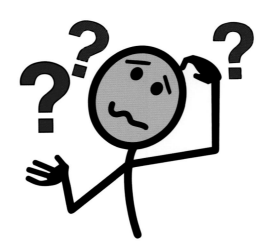

"What does it mean that someone has cancer?"

That is my first question. It has an answer.

Our bodies are made up of organs, and each organ has its own important job to do! The heart pumps blood, muscles make our arms and legs move, and our stomach helps us digest food. Even our skin is an organ!

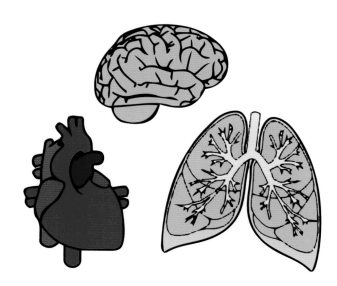

Every organ is made up of lots and lots of tiny cells. They're so small we can't even see them without a microscope! Just like organs, each cell has a job to do. When cells are finished with their job, our bodies clear them out and make new cells. That is how our bodies stay healthy and strong.

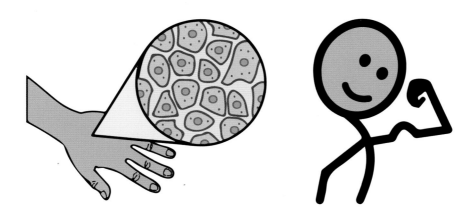

When someone has cancer, it means that some cells are not doing the job they are supposed to do. Those cells are not cleared out by the person's body, and they take up too much space from the healthy cells. They also might become a different size or shape, or even end up in the wrong place.

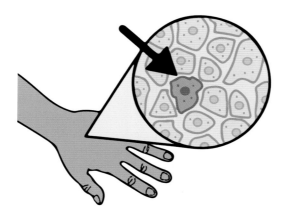

There are many kinds of cancer, depending on which cells are not doing their job.

Next I want to know, **"How do people get cancer?"**

People get cancer for different reasons, but a lot of the time we just don't know why someone's cells stop doing their job. It's hard not knowing the answer to that, but I learn it's not their fault that they got cancer.

"Can I catch cancer?" I ask. I am getting worried. I spend a lot of time with this person and now they have cancer!

No. Cancer is not like a cold, or other germs that you need to be careful about. Nobody can catch cancer from another person, no matter how much time they spend together.

When I'm sick, I go to the doctor and I take medicine for a few days. **"Do people with cancer also take medicine?"** I wonder.

I learn that medicine for cancer is different from things that I've had medicine for, like a sore throat or an ear infection. People with cancer often take medicine or have treatments with big names, like chemotherapy or radiation therapy.

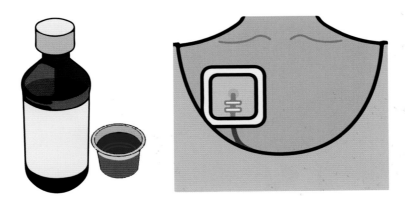

They might get the medicine through something called a port. Since nobody likes to get poked with a needle, a port gets medicine right into the body without having to use a needle each time.

Then I learn something really strange.
The medicine can make people with cancer feel
sicker! It might make them extra tired, or even
throw up. Yuck!

"Why would people take medicine that makes them feel sicker?" Of course, that's my next question!

It turns out the medicine that helps get rid of the cancer cells also takes away some of the healthy cells. That can make someone feel yucky for a while.

I learn another big word: side-effect. That's when something that's supposed to be helpful causes other problems.

Even though that's a question with an answer, it still feels confusing. So I ask my next question:

"If someone I love has cancer, will I make them sicker if I get too close to them?"

Not usually. Sometimes, if I have a cold or I don't feel well, I might have to be careful that I don't share my germs with the person who has cancer. Since their body is working to get rid of the cancer cells, it can be harder to make a cold go away.

"When someone has cancer, do they still look and act the same?"

The person will always be that same person I loved before they got cancer. They might look tired because their body is working hard to get better, or act grumpy if they don't feel so well. They might become thinner or heavier because of certain medicines. They also might lose their hair. That's another side-effect of the medicine. It doesn't hurt people to lose their hair, but that could make them look really different.

I also hear people talking about surgery. I wonder if there is something else wrong. **"Do all people with cancer have surgery?"** I ask.

I learn that a lot of people with cancer have surgery in a hospital. Since the cancer cells are not doing their job anymore, it can be helpful to take them out. Some people need to have one surgery, and other people need to have a few different surgeries. It depends on the kind of cancer, and what doctors think is best.

I might need to be more gentle after someone has surgery, and be careful about how tightly I hug them.

But I don't need to be afraid that I'm going to hurt the person I love, even if they have surgery. They will tell me if there's something that hurts them, and I'll be sure not to touch them there. I can still sit next to them and we can still be together.

I'm getting the idea that cancer is really different from when I get sick and have to go to the doctor. I start to wonder, **"Can someone die from cancer?"**

Yes, but many people don't die from cancer. Some people have cancer for a short amount of time and then get better, and other people live with cancer for a long time and keep taking medicine. I learn that the grown-ups will help me know what to expect.

I like things the way they are. I know what to expect and I know what happens every day. So I ask, **"Are my days going to be different because someone I love has cancer?"**

I find out that even though some big things are happening, not *everything* is going to change.

They might not be able to go swimming with me, or drive me to school, or they might get tired before we finish a game. But they still love me and I still love them.

Sometimes there are a lot of people around when someone has cancer. They want to visit and try to help. It can feel busy and people might try to hug me a lot. I don't have to ask about any of that. I see it for myself!

Now I know it's okay for me to take a break, or go to a quiet space and come back when I feel ready. I also know that if the person who has cancer doesn't live in my home, I might be able to go visit them or draw them a picture, and be one of the helpers.

This is a lot of stuff to think about at one time. **"What will it feel like for me when someone I love has cancer?"**

I learn it can feel scary for kids and for grown-ups. I might cry. It's okay to cry when I feel sad. Even grown-ups might cry.

Sometimes I might feel confused or angry that someone I love has cancer. But I won't always feel those things and neither will the grown-ups. People with cancer and the people who love them can be happy, too!

It's okay if I want to talk about the person I love
who has cancer, and it's also okay if I don't.

Even though some things are going to be different, lots of things will stay the same. I will have regular days again. I will still wake up, eat my breakfast, and go to school. I will know what to expect every day. I will try to be flexible when things don't go exactly as planned.

I might think of more questions to ask. Now I know that a lot of my questions will have answers, but some of them won't.

Most days are regular days. Most days I know just what to expect. Today was not a regular day, but I learned a lot. Mostly I learned that asking questions really helps!

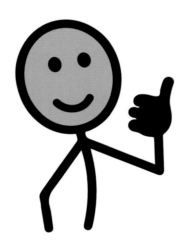

Short Picture Story:
I Have a Question about Cancer

On the pages that follow, you will see the same pictures used in the story along with shorter, more direct text. This is a tool for children who learn best through visual cues, and for children who might want to re-read and think about the story independently.

Hi!

I like games.

I like swimming.

I like watching my favorite show.

Most days are the same.

I go to school.

I see my friends.

I come home at the end of the day.

Today is different. Someone I love has cancer.

I have a lot of questions.

What does it mean that someone has cancer?

Some cells in their body are not doing their job.

How do people get cancer?

There are lots of different reasons people get cancer,

but we usually don't know why.

Can I catch cancer?

No, I can't catch cancer.

Do people with cancer take medicine?

Yes. It is very different from medicine I take.

Some cancer medicine can make people feel sicker.

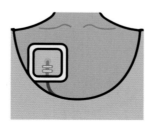

Why would people take medicine that makes them feel sicker?

The medicine that takes away the cancer cells also takes away some healthy cells.

If someone I love has cancer, will I make them sicker if I get too close to them?

No, but if I don't feel well I shouldn't share my germs with them.

When someone has cancer, do they still look and act the same?

They might look thinner or heavier.

Their hair might fall out.

But they're still the same person.

Do all people with cancer have surgery?

A lot of people with cancer have one or more surgeries.

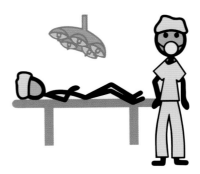

Can someone die from cancer?

Yes, but many people don't die from cancer.

Are my days going to be different?

Lots of things will stay the same, even if we can't do all the things together that we did before.

They still love me and I still love them.

There might be more people around and they might want to hug me. I can take a break.

I can draw a picture or be a helper.

What will it feel like when someone I love has cancer?

I might feel sad, confused or angry.

I won't always feel those things.

Lots of things will stay the same. I will have regular days again.

Asking questions really helps!

Suggestions for Parents and Caregivers

The following are suggestions to support a child, including one with special needs, through the process of a loved one having cancer.

Communicating with the child

Talking to children about a loved one with cancer may feel daunting; even the word "cancer" can evoke strong emotions and associations for many people. However, often it can be scarier for a child to *sense* that something is going on, but not be told explicitly. Use honest, clear language, parceling out information as they are able to process it. Since many children are concrete thinkers, try to avoid euphemisms, such as, "They're under the weather." A clearer alternative may be, "They have an illness called cancer." Describing where the cancer is and how doctors are helping to treat it will also help make the topic more concrete.

Addressing concerns about cancer

Some children worry they caused the person's cancer, or are in some way responsible. Adults can provide reassurance that there is nothing the child said or did to cause the cancer, there is nothing they can do to fix it, and they cannot "catch" it. Children are likely to worry about someone dying from cancer, even if they don't ask. Parents and caregivers can talk about that fear, and share that many people who have cancer live a long life, but it is possible to die from cancer. Reassure them that doctors do their very best to find the right treatment so that people can get better.

Preparing the child for changes with the person

Try to anticipate some of the physical changes that may be occurring. Many children have questions about hair falling out, a port in someone's chest, or other changes in appearance. If the person is having surgery, let the child know they might not be able to hug them tightly or sit on their lap, and the person might be tired. Explore ways the child might be helpful, such as bringing the person a drawing, or watching TV next to them.

Paying attention to structure and routine

Many children have difficulty with changes in routine. If the person with cancer is a primary caregiver, a sibling, or someone else who lives in the child's home, the daily schedule and roles of family members may change for short or long periods of time. Help the child anticipate these changes as best as possible, and use a calendar or picture schedule to provide guidance and reassurance about the daily routine. If the person with cancer lives outside of the home, explain that the child might not see them as much as usual. Reassure the child that even when someone has cancer, there will always be a daily routine and plan.

Supplying sensory-based supports

As the child works to process and cope with this new information, think about strategies that have been comforting in the past. Consider having available a quiet space, sensory-friendly toys, or other tools that have worked in new or challenging situations.

Providing emotional guidance

Know ahead of time that children, including those with special needs, may regress or turn to self-soothing behaviors as they cope with a loved one having cancer. Some children may become more withdrawn, irritable, anxious, or aggressive. Help them recognize their feelings, and provide messages of unconditional love. Reassure the child that it is ok to play, laugh, and do activities that are fun when someone has cancer. Partner with other adults in their life, such as teachers, counselors, or therapists, to help support them during this time.

Arlen Grad Gaines is a licensed clinical social worker based in Maryland, USA. With over a decade's experience in hospice social work, she has developed a specialization in supporting families who have children with special needs around the subject of grief and loss.

Meredith Englander Polsky has been working in social work and special education for almost 20 years and lives in Maryland, USA. She founded Matan, Inc. (www.matankids.org) in 2000, which has helped improve Jewish education around special needs for tens of thousands of families.